The 'all' Wall
VI

By Viola & Zaida Stefano

VeeZee Publications

Copyright © VeeZee Publications Pty. Ltd. 2025
First published in Australia in 2025
by VeeZee Publications Pty. Ltd.
veezeepublications.com

The right of Viola Stefano to be identified as the author of this work have been asserted by her in accordance with the **Copyright Amendment (Moral Rights) Act 2000.**

All rights reserved. Apart from any use as permitted by the author & under the **Copyright Act 1968**, no part may be reproduced, copied, scanned, stored in a retrieval system, recorded, or shared, by any means or in any form, without prior written & signed authorization from the publisher.

ISBN: 978-1-923120-17-4

A catalogue record of this book is available from the **National Library of Australia.**

Author: Viola Stefano
Illustrations, cover & internal designs: Zaida Stefano

Illustrations copyright © Zaida Stefano 2025
Design copyright © Zaida Stefano 2025

Disclaimer: The content presented in this book is meant for educational purposes only. The author & publisher claim no accountability to any entity or person for any liability, damage, or loss caused or assumed to be caused directly or indirectly as a consequence of the application, use, or interpretation of the material in this book.

Core words used in this book

I	want	can	stop	look
like	more	he	go	see
here	what	do	the	and
out	where	we	it	up
not	they	when	that	down
she	now	them	is	put
help	off	you	yes	on
turn	who	this	no	why
done	make	a	to	under
come	in	some	which	there
open	get	good	same	home

This flower is small, and that one is tall.

You like the small, and I like the tall.

She likes that small one close to the wall.

He likes the flowers close to the hall.

They are all blue, and all very tall.

These are all white, and all very small.

Here is the wind, and some of them fall.

They roll on the ground like that little red ball.

"Stop!" you call, "let no more fall!"

I like the flowers when they are tall.

You like the flowers when they are small.

Words with 'all' in this book

all	call	tall
hall	wall	ball
small	fall	

We hope you had fun reading!

Learning made easy with VeeZee

VeeZee Publications

Wait, there's more!

Visit our website for information about our range of readers & supporting products.

veezeepublications.com

www.ingramcontent.com/pod-product-compliance
Lightning Source LLC
Chambersburg PA
CBHW041154070526
44584CB00004B/300